D1591625

IMAGES
of America

UNITED STATES
DISCIPLINARY BARRACKS

USDB PLOT PLAN

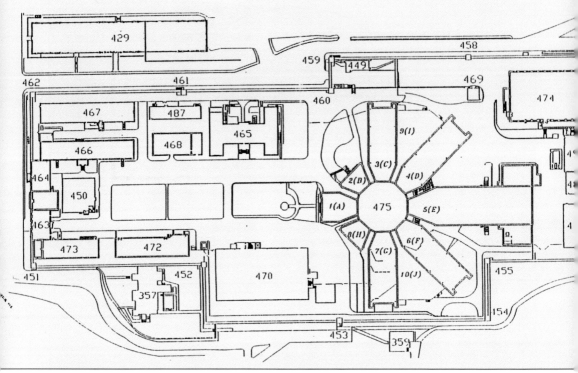

This diagram depicts the United States Disciplinary Barracks Castle and surrounding buildings with associated building numbers. These building numbers are annotated with picture captions throughout the book.

IMAGES
of America

UNITED STATES
DISCIPLINARY BARRACKS

Peter J. Grande

ARCADIA
PUBLISHING

Published by Arcadia Publishing
Charleston, South Carolina

Printed in the United States of America

Library of Congress Control Number: 2009930407

For all general information contact Arcadia Publishing at:
Telephone 843-853-2070
Fax 843-853-0044
E-mail sales@arcadiapublishing.com
For customer service and orders:
Toll-Free 1-888-313-2665

Visit us on the Internet at www.arcadiapublishing.com

OPINIONS EXPRESSED IN THIS BOOK ARE THOSE OF THE AUTHOR
AND DO NOT NECESSARILY REPRESENT THE POSITION OF THE
UNITED STATES ARMY OR THE DEPARTMENT OF DEFENSE.

CONTENTS

ACKNOWLEDGMENTS

My name appears on this book's cover, but the credit belongs to all the individuals over the years who took the pictures and documented the history of the United States Disciplinary Barracks (USDB) in the annual historical summaries; they are the ones who made this book possible. This pictorial history of the USDB would still be a vision without the motivation, technical skill, and infectious enthusiasm of the following individuals: Fred Bond, James Gray, Michelle Grier, Ann Grove, John Hughey, and Patricia Weishaar, USDB; Ken LaMaster, United States Penitentiary Leavenworth; Laura Phillipi, Lansing Historical Museum; and Russ Ronspies and George Moore, Frontier Army Museum. A special thanks to my wife, Fely, who endured the separation while I spent long hours researching, writing, and editing this manuscript. Thanks go to all those who ever served at the USDB.

Unless otherwise noted, all images appear courtesy of the USDB archives.

INTRODUCTION

In 1870, Maj. Thomas F. Barr was serving as the judge advocate of the east attending the first conference of the American Correctional Association (formerly the National Prison Association) in Cincinnati with wardens, superintendents, reformatory board members, and general philanthropists. He alerted the secretary of war to the poor and inhumane conditions of military prisoners. Military prisoners were confined at over 30 different stockades and penitentiaries throughout the United States. The treatment of these prisoners varied and included branding, wearing of striped uniforms, regimental shackling, and beatings. The secretary of war formed a delegation to investigate. The delegation inspected military prisoner locations and visited the British Military Confinement Facilities in Canada, resulting in the recommendation to establish a military prison system. The U.S. Army and the House Military Committee could not agree on the location for the first military prison with several options discussed: Fort Wood or Lafayette in New York Harbor and Rock Island Arsenal in Illinois. On March 3, 1873, an act was approved to establish a military prison at Rock Island and to use inmate labor at the arsenal. The U.S. Army objected and identified the shortfalls and dangers of using inmate labor at an arsenal and proposed a different site. On May 21, 1874, Congress approved to amend the act for the military prison to be established at Rock Island, Illinois, and directed it be established at Fort Leavenworth, Kansas. The amendment further provided that the government buildings on Fort Leavenworth be modified and used as practicable for the purpose of a military prison.

Twice in its history, the military prison was transferred to the United States Department of Justice and was used as a prison for civil offenders. It was first transferred in 1895 and then back to the U.S. Army in 1906. During this period, the Department of Justice used the military prisoners to build the United States Penitentiary. In 1915, between transfers to the Department of Justice by an act of Congress, the military prison's name was changed from the United States Military Prison to the United States Disciplinary Barracks (USDB). In 1929, the institution was once again transferred to the Department of Justice, at which time it was re-designated as the Leavenworth Penitentiary Annex. The military prisoners remained confined at this institution during these periods of Department of Justice control. In November 1940, the prison was reestablished as the USDB and has since been operated by the Department of the Army.

Since the establishment of the United States Military Prison in 1874, a unit has been responsible for providing prisoner supervisors and support personnel. Among the early predecessors of the 705th Military Police Battalion were the Disciplinary Guard Battalion; the 1st Guard Company; HHC, USDB; and through much of its history, simply the Guard. The 40th Military Police Battalion was activated on April 15, 2009, and relieved the 705th Military

Police Battalion of their USDB duties in preparation for their deployment to support Operation Enduring Freedom.

On April 5, 1994, the secretary of the army made the decision to build a new USDB, with a capacity for 510 inmates. A cost ceiling of $63 million in allocated construction dollars was set. The target budget year for funding this project was fiscal year 1998. Construction began in the summer of 1998, with completion projected for late summer 2001. The groundbreaking ceremony for the new USDB was held on June 12, 1998, with the keys handed over to Fort Leavenworth on August 1, 2002. After training and certifying the staff, the process to transfer the staff and inmates to the new facility began. A ribbon-cutting ceremony took place on September 20, 2002, and the first inmates arrived from the old USDB on September 30, 2002. Between September 30 and October 5, 2002, using a prison bus from the United States Penitentiary-Leavenworth, all the inmates were transferred from the old USDB to the new USDB. It took approximately eight years and six months to complete the mission after the secretary of the army directed a new USDB be built. On Saturday, October 5, 2002, at 1322 hours, the USDB Emergency Operation Center sent the following e-mail message, "Mission complete, all inmates are secure and all routes are open. CMC Per Order CPT Washington." At 1700, the same day, a flag detail led by S.Sgt. Barbara Fletcher retired the national colors from the old USDB for the last time. The colors are displayed in the showcase at the new USDB.

On August 16, 2004, demolition started on the "Castle" at the old USDB. The destruction began on five wing, and on January 9, 2005, three wing was the last remaining structure torn down. An estimated 6,000 truckloads of debris were removed from the area to be recycled or taken to the landfill.

The USDB is the only maximum-security correctional facility in the Department of Defense (DoD), and the oldest penal institution in the federal system. The USDB staff includes members of the MP corps, adjutant general corps, medical corps, medical service corps, corps of engineers, chaplain corps, judge advocate general corps, the United States Marine Corps, the United States Air Force, and the United States Navy, working to achieve a progressive correctional community.

The USDB's motto, "Our Mission, Your Future," symbolizes the "Can Do" attitude, the spirit of teamwork, and the philosophy of the USDB. The entire custodial staff provides individualized treatment to inmates to prepare them for a self-reliant, trustworthy, and respectable future. The USDB reflects on the past only to build for the future, emphasizing behavior, education, vocational skills, and a chance to choose.

One

ESTABLISHMENT OF A UNITED STATES MILITARY PRISON

The purchase of the Louisiana Territory opened new lands extending from the Mississippi River to the Rocky Mountains. The U.S. Army established cantonments and forts along the rivers and trails to protect traders and settlers. Col. Henry Leavenworth and soldiers from the Third U.S. Infantry established Fort Leavenworth in May 1827. Located on the high bluffs on the west of the Missouri river, it provided oversight and protection of the river below. As the trade increased across the plains, Fort Leavenworth became an important quartermaster point for settlers taking the long the journey on the Oregon, California, and Santa Fe Trails. (Courtesy Army Frontier Museum.)

This picture is a view of the northwest corner of the quartermaster depot. Building 467 constructed in 1887 is a four-story building and is inside the walls. The two buildings located outside the walls of the depot commissary are currently the site of building 429, which houses the 40th and 705th Military Police Battalions (internment and resettlement). (Courtesy Army Frontier Museum.)

Brig. Gen. (then Maj.) Thomas F. Barr is considered the "Father of the USDB." In 1870, while serving as the judge advocate of the east, he identified the horrible conditions of military prisoners confined at stockades and state penitentiaries. He stayed active in military penal reform until his retirement on May 22, 1901. The U.S. Army, as a farewell gift for his long dedicated service to his country (including the Civil War), appointed and served as the Judge Advocate General on his retirement day.

Here are two views of the south wall and entrance into the quartermaster depot. On May 21, 1874, Congress approved to amend the act for the military prison to be established at Rock Island, Illinois, and directed it be established at the military reservation at Fort Leavenworth, Kansas. The quartermaster department was ordered to move its supply depot to the buildings of the Fort Leavenworth Arsenal. The archway in the picture below would become known as south gate, the main entrance into the United States Military Prison.

On June 30, 1895, the United States Military Prison ceased to exist under military control and was turned over to the Department of Justice and renamed the United States Penitentiary. On June 10, 1896, over 500 acres of land on the southern boundary of Fort Leavenworth reservation was transferred to the Department of Justice to build the penitentiary, workshops, and other buildings necessary to employ United States prisoners. Escapes were common during the forced marches to and from the work site.

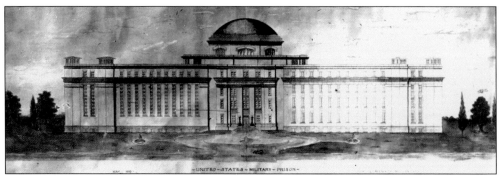

This May 1910 drawing of the proposed new military prison at Fort Leavenworth does not resemble the castle. The castle was built with the hub-and-spoke design with a central rotunda and eight radiating wings. The construction of the penitentiary was under the charge of F. E. Hines. A sawmill, brick plant, and a stone quarry were built to support the construction. In 1926, the dome over the rotunda was completed, thus the nickname the "Big Top." (Courtesy Army Frontier Museum.)

DRY KILN AT STOCKADE
UNITED STATES MILITARY PRISON
FT. LEAVENWORTH KAS.
JUNE 30 1910

The construction of the castle required millions of bricks. A brick plant was established near the current Sherman Army Airfield and sheets of clay were cut into brick size. These bricks were transported by rail to the construction site north of the old quartermaster depot. A picket was established on the cliff overlooking the plant to supervise the inmates working. The bricks shown in this June 30, 1910, photograph were probably used to build either the power plant or five wing of the castle. In the picture below, mule teams and wagons were used to transport the stones from the local quarry to the military prison. (Above, courtesy Army Frontier Museum.)

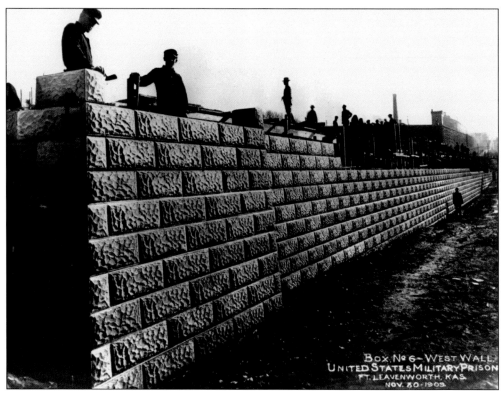

Seen here is the construction of the west wall in 1909 and the north wall in 1911. Cement blocks were used to build the walls, and with the terminal railway system completed, a switch was run directly into the prison. This saved recourses both in time and labor because mules and wagons were used to haul the cement blocks from the kilns. Soldiers were posted on both the inside and outside of the walls to prevent the prisoners from escaping.

In the Sundry Civil Appropriation Act approved May 27, 1908, $150,000 was allocated for reconstruction and the maximum use of employment of inmates was to be used. A detail plan was prepared in the office of the quartermaster general and was approved by the prison board and the secretary of war. Construction on five wing started in 1909 and was completed in 1913. The entire construction of the castle was from 1909 to 1921.

Construction of four wing started in 1911 and was completed in 1914. The railroad tracks can be seen through the west gate entrance to the construction site. The ground preparation for three wing is between the wall separating the old quartermaster depot and the construction of the castle. The remaining wings of the castle and their completion dates are 1914, three wing; 1915, eight wing; 1916, seven wing; 1917, six wing; 1918, one wing; and 1921, two wing. (Courtesy Army Frontier Museum.)

The construction of the power plant started about the same time as five wing and was completed in 1911. Located northwest of the castle, it was built on some of the Bluntville land, but most of the houses were rebuilt and housed families of the soldiers working in the military prison. In the picture below, the smoke stack for the power plant was built in 1910. The power plant provided steam to the castle and other renovated buildings in the old quartermaster depot.

Supervisors of the military prisoners conducted accountability formations prior to and upon completion of work call. Prisoners would stand in formation by the detail that they were assigned to and account for. It was not uncommon for inmates to escape while on outside work details. Escaped inmates would be caught by the local populace and returned to the U.S. Army's control. In both pictures, inmates are standing with their arms folded across their chest. This may have been to keep them from putting their hands in their pockets.

Horse and buggy were the mode of transportation around the prison for inmate workers. The view is from south gate with building 472 on the right. In the below picture, buildings 473 (left) and 472 (right) can be seen inside the wall. A wagon with mules and a driver positioned in front of building 357, the commandant's quarters was used to take him to meetings on the installation or to visit the USDB farm or other locations inmates were working.

The mode of transportation for the military prison changed over time. Mules and wagons gave way to the horseless carriage, and a garage was established to perform maintenance. Automobile engine repair would become a vocational training program in the USDB. In the picture below, the railroad track to the power plant was still in operation.

Seen here is the construction of the castle, with three and four wings completed and overshadowing the west gate vehicle entrance. Notice the circular security shack to the right of the vehicle entrance. Nine tower and ten tower on top of west gate are brick with long vertical gun ports. These gun ports were later replaced with larger windows to increase the visibility of the soldiers in the towers. Seven wing was still under construction and not complete until 1917.

Building 468, built in 1878, had a steam boiler and piped steam to the old quartermaster depot buildings. It later became the hub for the complex tunnel system under the prison for the steam pipes from the power plant. Once the new power plant was finished, this building was used as a machine shop for steam piping.

Here are two views of the construction of building 429. This three-story brick building was built as the barracks for the 1st Guard Company. The top two floors were used as squad bays for the soldiers. The first floor had administrative offices and a mess hall. The basement was for storage and an armory. (Courtesy Army Frontier Museum.)

This is a view from on top of two wing into the courtyard of the USDB on April 29, 1928. Building 10 was later destroyed, and the courtyard remained free of any buildings. In the below picture, the new hospital (building 465) was under construction and later completed in 1930. The new hospital provided a more sterile environment for the sick and wounded since all of its floors were made of concrete. The new hospital was designed with an elevator for easy transportation of inmate patients between floors. The old hospital, which was built in 1878, was renovated into vocational training shops.

The wooden wall was built as a temporary barrier until the rock wall was completed. The wooden wall bisects building 367, which was originally a storehouse and office for the quartermaster. In 1876, it was renovated to serve as the quarters for the prison governor and the prison surgeon. Several years later, the title *governor* was replaced with *commandant*. The west end (left) of the building was the quarters for the prison surgeon and provided him easy access to the prison hospital in building 472. For security reasons, it was thought best not to have part of the building inside the wall and the rest outside the wall. Once the stone wall was completed, the portion of the building inside the wall was removed, and in the 1880s, an addition was added to the east end. Capt. James W. Pope was commandant for eight years, and he and his wife had the reputation of extravagant and lively parties and entertainment. The commandant's tour of duty is now limited to two years.

Built between 1855 and 1859, building 367 is one of the oldest structures on Fort Leavenworth. Located at 20 Riverside Avenue, it is now the quarters of the USDB commandant. The building sits on a limestone foundation and has a seam metal roof. This two-story quarters has prominent gabled pediment with pronounced returns and the molded cornice parallel Greek Revival design. The south entrance and the porch have a recessed gabled pediment and are consistent with the Greek Revival style. In 1876, the heavily molded double doors, triple-sash fenestration, and wrap-around porch were influenced by Italianate architecture. This set of quarters is registered as a historical home and is maintained per the guidelines developed by the secretary of the interior. Since the screening on the porch was not within the guidelines it was removed. The below picture was taken of the quarters in 2008.

Two

THE UNITED STATES DISCIPLINARY BARRACKS

In 1915, by order of the secretary of war, the name and official designation of the United States Military Prison (USMP) was changed to the United States Disciplinary Barracks (USDB). Two-thirds of the prisoners were incarcerated for desertion, commonly known as "going over the hill." There was hope for restoration to the service for those soldiers, and the USDB was to instill discipline and vocational training. The majority of the soldiers who served their sentence did well upon their release, except for those who had been confined previously in a civilian penal institution.

The main entrance of the prison was called South Gate, with the big letters "U.S.D.B." over the archway. It has always raised a question from visitors as to why the year 1877 is above the South Gate. It does not represent the year the United States Military Prison or USDB was founded but is the date building 463 was built and South Gate runs through this building.

The symbolism on the USDB Distinctive Unit Insignia is the sun, which symbolizes authority, healing, knowledge, and a new beginning representing the overall mission of the organization. The sword denotes all military personnel. The oak leaves and columns refer to military and civilian stability in rehabilitation. The columns and inscribed scroll simulate a doorway and allude to the custodial guidance of the unit.

This view of the courtyard is from the one wing entrance of the castle toward the USDB's South Gate entrance. It has been said the sidewalk in this picture was built in the 1920s, and the design is similar to a hammer and sickle of the Russian Revolution.

This view is on the eighth tier of the rotunda of the castle with a security door with bars partly open. This photograph depicts the beautiful wood molding wrapped around the top of the rotunda. Security fencing was placed on each tier where the inmates had access to prevent inmates from attempting suicide by jumping.

Built in 1840, building 466 has three floors with continuous stone footings and brick and stone walls with wood beams. The ground floor was used for carpentry, paint, and masonry shops, while the two upper floors were used for inmate housing in dormitory and small room configurations. The back door to the vocational shop included a storage garage for a boat.

Building 467 was constructed in 1887 with four floors and continuous stone footings, brick and stone walls with wood beams. The plumbing and electrical shops were in the basement. The first floor was used by the furniture repair shop, and the second floor contained the Directorate of Inmate Administration, formerly named the Directorate of Classification. The top floor was the inmate craft shop divided into four separate hobby areas: wood making, ceramics with kilns, leather making, and canvas painting. During the summer of 1945, 14 German prisoners of war (POWs) were executed by hanging, and it is said to have been in the elevator shaft of this building. In the picture at right, an inmate worker stands in the doorway of the tool room.

The old mess hall in the castle was one large seating area where hundreds of inmates gathered three times per day. Painted on the wall were the following two statements: "Everything on your plate shall be eaten—No food will be wasted" and "Do not accept more food than you can eat—Eat all you accept."

Because of the risk of massing large number of inmates in the mess hall, five wing's dining area was later renovated into two separate areas. The signs above the door state "Are you sure you turned in your silverware" and "Attention, 1. Stay behind line until 'walk' light is on. 2. Walk through metal detector slowly placing left foot inside painted box on floor. 3. Do not touch metal detector."

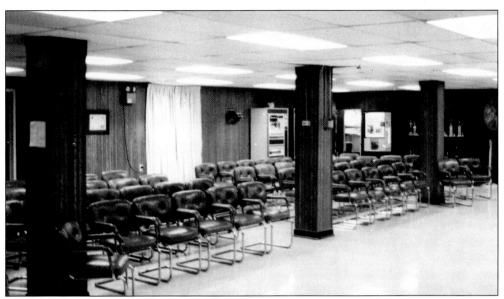

The inmate visitation room was located on the first floor of building 463, to the east of the south gate entrance. The USDB encouraged visitation by family and friends to maintain the morale of the inmates and to develop closer relationships between the inmate and family members. The vending machines were provided for the visitors and inmates during daily visitation. Inmate visitation was during the evenings on weekdays and during the day on weekends and holidays. An initial embrace and kiss were authorized at the beginning and end of visitation. The visitation room was multipurpose, and the staff used it for training and briefings.

The outdoor recreation yard was outside the walls of the USDB, and the portal was a detention door in the north wall. The key to access the recreation yard was kept in six tower and the solider would lower the key to a staff member in a bucket. The yard consisted of a running track, softball field, basketball courts, tennis courts, handball courts, weight lifting equipment, and a latrine. During recreation times, soldiers armed with weapons would post in the five towers surrounding the recreation field.

Building 465 has four floors and was built in 1930 with reinforced concrete foundations and concrete floors with load-bearing brick walls. It was originally built in 1930 as a hospital for the inmates. The left side of the basement was the vocational barbershop, and the right side was the medical and dental clinics. The first floor was administrative offices, and in the picture below, the sign above the door reads "Board of Penal Institutions." The second and third floors were used to house inmates.

Inside the castle, there were many areas to accommodate the various inmate religions. The Catholic inmates met in this chapel named after Saint Dismas, also known as the "Good Thief" or "Penitent Thief," as described in the Gospel of Luke. The Bethany Fellowship volunteer group from the Fort Leavenworth Saint Ignatius Parish has been visiting inmates at the USDB for nearly 30 years.

This view is of the exterior wall of the first three tiers of one of the castle wings. The ladders on the wall were part of the emergency evacuation for those staff and inmates on the second tier of the castle base. The first two tiers of the castle housed the maximum custody and death sentenced inmates. This access from the castle base was always a security concern to the USDB staff.

The command judge advocate's office was located in building 473. This building was constructed in 1865 with a continuous stone footing with brick load-bearing walls and wood beams. This legal office provided assistance to inmates for civil legal issues such as divorce, wills, power of attorney, and notary services. Lawsuits against the commandant were also tracked.

Constructed in 1972, building 450 was the newest building within the walls. It had a steel frame with concrete floors and concrete block walls. The offices and group treatment rooms for the Directorate of Treatment Programs, formerly named the Directorate of Mental Health were in this building. After the move to the new USDB, this building was infested with mold and was destroyed.

This view is from the north end of the old quartermaster depot. The large building on the right did not survive over time. This view of the courtyard was prior to the construction of the castle. Building 357, the USDB commandant's quarters can be seen outside the USDB wall. Building 468 in the below picture did survive the test of time. Constructed in 1878, it is one floor with continuous stone footings and stone-bearing walls. The pipefitting shop, or machine shop, has access to the massive tunnel system below the USDB.

This view is of the main control room in the rotunda of the castle. In the background is the entrance to three wing and limestone benches with No. 10 cans from the dining facility. The benches were used by inmates who were waiting to speak with the guard commander (now called the watch commander) because they were in some sort of trouble. The No. 10 cans were used for cigarette disposal. The security requirement to have improved visibility of the inmate necessitated the renovation of a second floor. No smoking is authorized in the new USDB.

The completed renovation of the second floor was completed, but over time, it did not provide the required security and was too small for the computer-driven electronic security systems. The below picture is of a new completed main control room in the castle rotunda. The second story included monitors to view all of the close circuit television cameras in the castle and the control panel to operate the electronic doors to the eight wings and two exterior doors of the castle.

The Local Parolee Unit (LPU), formerly known as the Local Parolee Company, was established on Sherman Heights in 1954. The LPU is three quarters of a mile northwest of the USDB with 19 buildings consisting of 11 barracks, three latrines, chapel, orderly room, supply room, mess hall, pool hall, visitors room, and an athletics area. Prior to the LPU, the Military Training Company was housed there for inmates approved by the U.S. Army and U.S. Air Force for restoration to the military service.

On April 5, 1965, a new LPU, later renamed Trusty Unit (TU), was completed. It consisted of an administration building, mess hall, and barracks. A recreation area was completed with sufficient room for various types of athletics and a picnic area. Several years later, a concrete hardstand was added to provide for basketball and volleyball. The TU is still operational today. A work release program was established to provide community-based employment on a conditional and part-time basis for selected inmates. These inmates were employed as cooks, mechanics, body repairmen, and general assembly workers in the local communities.

A winter ice storm turned the pine tree in front of the castle into an icicle wonderland, but it also caused havoc on the USDB infrastructure. An exterior metal door in the eastern wall of the South Gate area was frozen shut. The standing operating procedure was to melt the ice and perform a function check on the locking device. Some inmates at the USDB experienced their first taste of winter and Jack Frost.

For security reasons, security towers should be accessible from outside so soldiers do not have to bring weapons and ammunition inside the USDB. Though 11 of the 12 towers were designed that way, eight tower was not. The reason is a mystery. Some say the tower is haunted with ghosts, and the decision was made not to renovate it. Even though the tower has been abandoned for years, there are many different eight tower ghost stories. Some say the soldiers in other security towers reported seeing a person holding a gun while others say they received phone calls from the tower despite it not being manned. The phone seen below was found in the USDB archives, and it is believed to have been removed from the tower to stop the phone calls.

Three

LIFE INSIDE THE CASTLE

The purposes of post-trial confinement at the USDB per the Department of Defense policy are incapacitation, rehabilitation, deterrence, and punishment of prisoners. The USDB's motto is "Our Mission, Your Future" and the facility is operated with a "corrective" not "punitive" philosophy. Inmates are sentenced to the USDB as punishment and not for punishment. Life inside the castle is to prepare them to return to duty or civilian life with the prospect of becoming a productive individual.

This massive stone-and-brick wall is nine stories high and is one of the wings of the castle. Inmates did not have windows in their cells; instead, they received natural light from the large windows. Most of the inmates lived in general population single cells and were assigned a work detail. Inmates made choices to attend general and crime specific treatment programs, recreation activities, religious services, and educational opportunities.

The USDB operated on a strict schedule of calls, but free time in the housing unit day rooms was abundant. Inmates could watch television, play table tennis or board games, or just relax in their cell or at the dayroom tables.

There was an average of three correctional specialists to 240 inmates per general population housing unit. Soldiers were always vigilant in their duties conducting checks of each cell on all six tiers every 30 minutes. It takes a corrections trained professional to walk those tiers alone among the military's most violent offenders. Armed with only a radio, flashlight, and a pen, soldiers relied on their interpersonal communicative skills and self-defense techniques taught at the United States Army Military Police School.

Inmates in a general population housing unit are relaxing during an open recreation call. The rule for watching television was the majority of the inmates had to agree on what program they would watch. This proved to be difficult, and as a result of the growth of television stations, additional televisions were installed.

Soldiers are seen standing at the doors of the satellite dining area constructed adjacent to the housing unit. Supervising the movement in and out of the dining area was paramount in order to account for the meal utensils. Satellite dining was discontinued, and the dining areas were converted into dayrooms.

There are plenty of horror stories of the terrible food fed to inmates in prisons. But the quality and quantity of the food served at the USDB was good. The USDB dining facilities were operated by trained quartermaster soldiers with inmate assistants. The USDB leadership was aware that poor food service could lead to disgruntled inmates. The USDB staff consumed the same meals as the inmates. Seen at right, below, is a view of the dining facility after an inmate was allowed to paint a full wall mural. The pictures depict the different landscapes of America.

The outdoor recreation yard was the location where the inmates could blow off some excess energy. Using the skills taught in the masonry vocational shop, inmate workers constructed a concrete foundation for the basketball, volleyball, tennis, and handball courts. In the picture below, inmates relaxed on the large recreation yard by playing softball, flag football, running track, or just laying around after a hard day's work.

The sports detail No. 46 was active in power lifting competitions. In 1963, inmates from the USDB formed Amateur Athletic Union weight lifting teams. The USDB sponsored a team called the "Power Gang," which traveled throughout Kansas and in 1994 placed first in the state and regional power lifting meets. Various physical conditioning programs were implemented over the years such as boxing, wrestling, and gymnastics. On February 13, 1956, a trampoline was installed in the USDB gymnasium. In the 1960s, inmate variety shows occurred three to four times per year. These events were conducted on the stage in the five wing gymnasium. In 1962, two dramatic productions, *Mr. Roberts* and *My Three Angels*, were presented through the courtesy of the Fort Leavenworth Dramatics Club.

The USDB monthly inmate publication, *Stray Shots*, was written and produced by an inmate staff with oversight of USDB staff and contained nonfiction articles covering fields of entertainment, sports, and science. In the May 26, 1947, issue, an inmate wrote an article how he found a copy of the February 19, 1916, issue of *Stray Shots* in the wall of seven base in the castle. In this issue, the chaplain of the institution was the editor, and the inmate population was 1,049. In the 1980s, the name was changed to the *Trojan*. The current inmate publication is called *Passing Time*.

This December 31, 1913, picture depicts the band of the 1st Disciplinary Battalion, United States Military Prison. They are wearing a patch on their left sleeve, depicting a B within a circle. In the 1960s, the USDB Band was primarily a combination dance- and western-style organization with some progress towards a concert band. The band would play at outside engagements, and the funds would be placed in the Inmate Welfare Fund. The band also played at USDB functions such as sports events, banquets, graduation exercises, and variety shows. The band was discontinued in 1998 as part of the scale down in preparation to move to the new USDB.

The USDB maintained a recreation library and a law library. The library was open daily with a large selection of fiction, non-fiction, magazines, and newspapers. Inmates could relax and read in the library or check out books to read in their cell. The return book rate was excellent because the staff knew where to find an inmate with an overdue book.

Security was still the No. 1 priority inside the castle. Prior to the 1970s, female staff members were not allowed into the castle unless escorted by a male staff member. This allowed for the searching of inmates in the rotunda area. These four inmates were suspected of having contraband, and the decision was made to inspect them immediately. Soldiers conduct a systematic search starting with a frisk search and then each item of clothing. Female correctional specialists arrived at the USDB for duty in the early 1970s, and in May 1975, the first female inmates arrived and were billeted in building 465. In 1986, seven base of the castle was renovated to allow all female custody levels to be housed in one area. The U.S. Army and the U.S. Navy signed an agreement to confine female inmates at the Naval Consolidated Brig in Miramar, California, and on May 21, 2000, the female inmates were transferred.

Keys, locks, bars, and chains are common sights at the USDB. Opening and closing doors with large detention keys was a basic skill for correctional specialist, also known by the slang term "turnkey." A key control system was established to preclude having keys for interior doors on the same key ring as keys to exterior doors. Key inventory and accountability were conducted at least three times per day during the change of relief. In the picture below, a correctional specialist has positive control of the belly chain around the inmate's waist as he escorts the inmate to the bus that will transport him to the new USDB.

A typical general population single cell prior to the 1980s is seen here. The cell has a hardened china sink and toilet, bunk with mattress and drawer underneath, and a table legged locker. In the 1980s, a metal shelf was affixed to the wall toward the back of the cell, and the metal locker was replaced with a solid floor model. Additionally a wooden writing surface was affixed to the wall that would fold down when not in use.

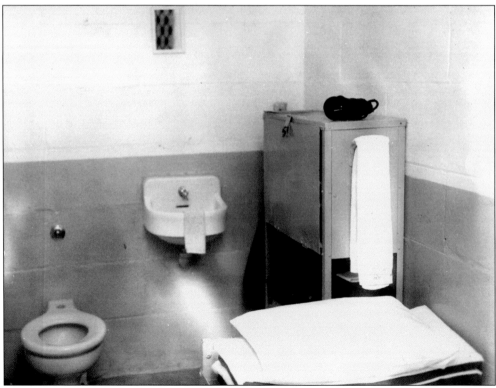

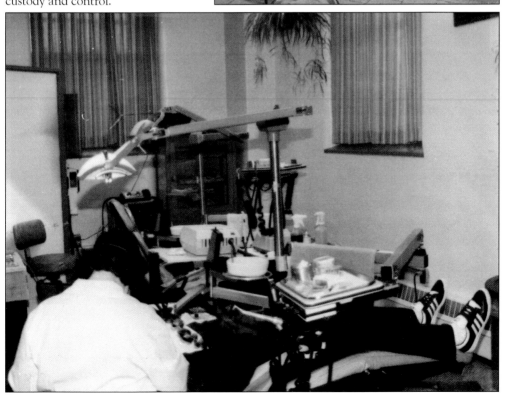

There were medical and dental services provided to the inmates in building 465. If the inmate's medical condition required a higher level of care, he was transported to the Munson Army Hospital on Fort Leavenworth. Ward 2B was designated as a prison ward, and inpatient care was provided by the hospital staff with USDB correctional specialists providing the custody and control.

To maintain discipline and order in the USDB, inmates were issued a rulebook. Some of the general rules changed, such as "Be quiet everywhere and at all times" and "You will be known by number while here." One rule that did not change is "When orders conflict obey the last one given you." An inmate is read charges of alleged infractions of the Manual for the Guidance of Inmates. If he is found guilty, he could lose privileges or be placed in disciplinary segregation. In the picture below, an inmate has nearly successfully completed his confinement. He is being measured for civilian clothing for his release.

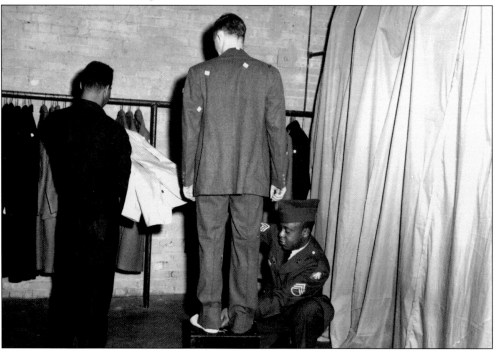

Four

DISORDERS, ESCAPES, AND EXECUTIONS

Thick black smoke filled the sky above the castle on April 27, 1997. It was not a disturbance or riot but a fire on the roof of five wing. At 1705 hours, a soldier reported smoke and immediately an emergency action plan was implemented. The on duty control room staff contacted the Fort Leavenworth Fire Department, provost marshal office, and USDB leadership while making an initial assessment of the situation. Immediately the staff prepared the inmates for evacuation from the castle to the different predetermined destinations within the walls of the USDB.

The Fort Leavenworth Fire Department, with assistance from the Kickapoo Fire Department and the Delaware Township Fire Department, responded. The fire was extinguished at approximately 1830 hours and was limited to the five wing roof and to the gymnasium immediately below. Three soldiers and two inmates suffered minor smoke inhalation and were treated and released from medical facilities. The fire was in the area where civilian contractors were making repairs to the roof. The mass evacuation of the inmates from the castle was not needed because of the swift response of the fire departments.

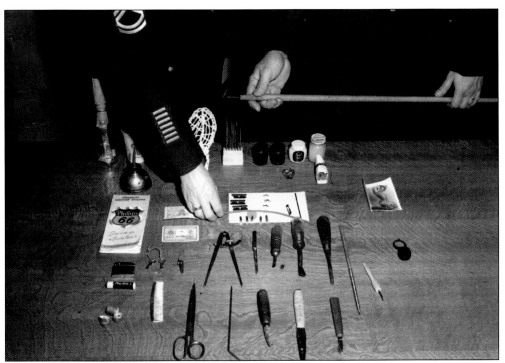

Contraband in the USDB is basically anything not authorized. Nuisance contraband is having over the limit of something that is authorized. Other contraband such as shanks (prison weapons), local maps, and flammable liquids are used by inmates for self-protection or to extort other inmates. The USDB staff members conduct daily searches of inmates leaving vocational training details and random cell and common area inspections.

Emergency action plans and drills were tested regularly in the USDB. Some of the emergency plans are for escapes, disturbances, taking of hostages, and severe weather. An emergency operation center (EOC) was activated when a situation threatened the USDB security. The EOC was located outside the USDB walls in the basement of building 429.

On March 2, 1996, a disturbance occurred in the castle's three wing housing unit with a correctional specialist being assaulted and held hostage. The inmates barricaded the entrance to the wing with lockers and desks, while arming themselves with chair legs, broom handles, and such. Soldiers equipped with disturbance gear entered the USDB in a formation similar to this picture and used high-pressure hoses and disturbance tactics to regain control. Four soldiers and three inmates were injured, and the damage to the wing was estimated at $10,000.

A forced cell move team (FCMT) is prepared to enter an inmate's cell. A FCMT is used when an inmate is a threat to himself or others and has refused an order to voluntarily be restrained. This five-member team is trained to use the minimum amount of force necessary to restrain the inmate. All FCMT are videoed to document the team's actions and to prepare a written report.

On August 17, 1987, during a security inspection behind building 470, a homemade wooden ladder, approximately four feet in length, was observed leaning against the wall behind the building with broken pieces of wood underneath. After a special count and thorough search of the USDB, it was determined that an inmate who worked on the wood shop detail had escaped. On August 22, 1987, he was apprehended in Kansas City, Missouri, by civilian authorities while taking coins from a water fountain in the Country Club Plaza.

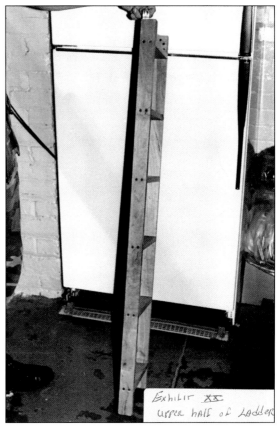

Exhibit XX
upper half of ladder

Exhibit VI
Exterior wall

59

On January 10, 1987, at 0030 hours, during a scheduled inmate count, two inmates were reported missing. The two inmates had escaped during the craft shop activity call on the evening of January 9, 1987. The inmates departed the castle during the craft shop call and proceeded to the south wall of the USDB, climbing the wall at the rear of building 464. The inmates proceeded over the first of three fences that placed them on the roof of the USDB Sales Store. After successfully negotiating the remaining two fences, they jumped down from the roof in a blind spot between towers 1 and 12. The inmates proceeded across McPherson Avenue and made their way to the railroad tracks east of the USDB. At 2344 hours, January 10, 1987, both inmates were captured at the Lorring Quarry in Bonner Springs, Kansas, by the Wyandotte County Sheriff's Department.

Most escapes in prison movies are through the vehicle gate. On April 30, 1998, at 1155 hours, during a scheduled inmate count, two inmates were reported missing. The two inmates hid in a trash compactor receptacle and escaped through the USDB west gate. The driver of the trash truck stopped at a convenient store in Platte County, Missouri, and a witness spotted the inmates getting out of the receptacle and running away. Law enforcement agencies established a perimeter of the area and started a systematic search. As deputies closed in on them, the inmates split up, and the deputies gave chase on foot. One inmate circled back to the patrol car and attempted to drive away. He refused orders to surrender and was shot twice by deputies. The other inmate was captured without incident.

U.S. Army policy authorized execution by musketry, hanging, and electrocution. There is no record of any executions by musketry or electrocution at the USDB. During 1945, 15 of the 97 military executions were conducted at the USDB including 14 German POWs. The last inmate executed at the USDB was on April 13, 1961. This was per the Department of the Army General Court-Martial order 37, dated July 17, 1957. He was sentenced to death for the rape and attempted premeditated murder of an 11-year-old Austrian girl.

The USDB Cemetery is located on Sheridan Drive, Fort Leavenworth. It is used for inmates who die while in the custody of the U.S. Army, and the inmate's family does not claim the body. The last person buried in the cemetery was executed at the USDB in 1957. The back row of the cemetery has the graves of the 14 German POWs who were sentenced to death by general courts-martial during World War II for killing fellow Germans in various POW camps across America.

There were no executions at the USDB using this electric chair. The origin of this electric chair is not documented in the USDB archives. Some say it was purchased from a state department of corrections, while others say it was built at Fort Leavenworth using blueprints. U.S. Army policy did mandate that executions by electrocution must be performed by a professional civilian executioner.

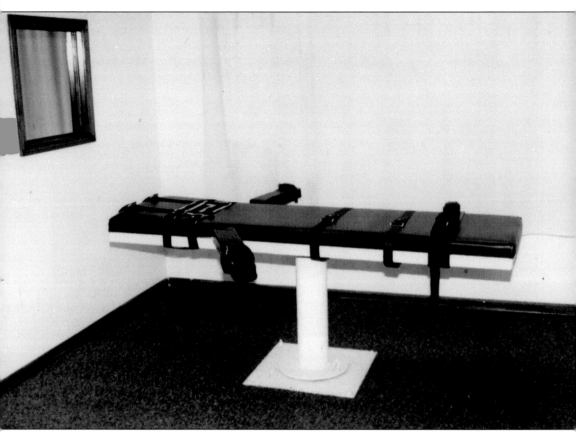

Current U.S. Army policy is for executions to be conducted by lethal injection. The president of the United States is the only person who can approve and order the execution of a death sentence under the Uniform Code of Military Justice and the Manual of Courts-Martial. This execution table was located on the first tier of two wing in the castle. The USDB commandant and a chaplain are the only two individuals authorized in the room with the condemned inmate during the execution.

Five

REHABILITATION
PROGRAMS

In 1877, the United States Military Prison (USMP) Shoe and Harness Shop were established as the first vocational training program for the inmates. At the end of the first year, the shop manufactured 39,880 pairs of shoes. Boots worn by soldiers were called "brogans," these were uncomfortable and poor in appearance; however, the shop supervisor made changes to the design, and it became the boot of choice. A report to the War Department criticized the boots made at the USMP as worthless because they fell apart after days of continuous marching. The report was not substantiated because the circumstances described in the report occurred during the campaign against Geronimo in the Arizona Territory.

U.S. Army policy mandated the commandant to employ inmates in labor and trades such as he deemed best for their health and reformation. Clean clothes and bedding were required to ensure a healthy environment where large numbers of persons are confined in limited space. The USDB like other correctional facilities had their own laundry and employed their inmates working there. The USDB used civilian and military supervisors qualified to instruct inmates on the proper use of the complex machines. Inmates are being instructed on how to use the blanket/linen folding machine.

A staff sergeant in the USDB Machine Shop is conducting a function check on a machine prior to the inmates arriving for work. Inmates and staff are required to wear personal protective equipment such as goggles when operating machines.

A soldier supervises an inmate conducting a project as part of the electrical vocational training program. Inmates were taught the basic electrical work, which gave them a skill to use upon release to civilian life.

The USDB automotive repair shop was located in building 496 and was a popular vocational training program. The shop repaired both military and civilian vehicles. The crawl, walk, run, process was used to teach inmates simple tasks like changing spark plugs to a complete overhaul of an engine. In the picture below, an inmate is disassembling a fuel pump for repair. Inmates were offered to test for the Automotive Services Excellence Certification upon completion of the classroom instruction and hands-on training.

The USDB automotive body shop was located in building 486 and offered formal classroom educational automobile body classes as well as on-the-job-training. Inmates could earn both a Kansas State Vocational Training Certificate and test for an Automotive Service Excellence Certificate. Inmates are sanding off the excess compound prior to the painting phase of the vehicles.

The USDB woodworking shop was located in building 467 and later moved to Pope Hall in 1963. Inmates were instructed in basic carpentry skills by certified instructors. The shop specialized in custom furniture. Some of the special orders were for Gen. Colin Powell, chairman of the Joint Chiefs of Staff and Gen. Carl Mundy, commandant of the U.S. Marine Corps. Inmates also made training aids for major army command, like drop leg tables in the picture below.

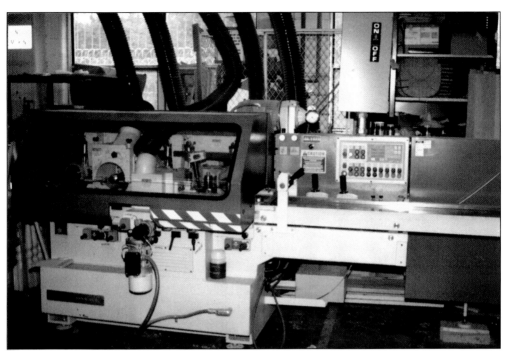

Historic homes on military installations are restored under the guidelines developed by the secretary of the interior. With the potential business for restoration of these homes, the woodworking shop purchased a five-head molder, knife grinder, and hydraulic duplicating lathe to facilitate the manufacturing of historically significant moldings and turnings. This shop provides decking for porches and spindles of historic homes on Fort Leavenworth; Fort Myers, Virginia; and Fort Bliss, Texas.

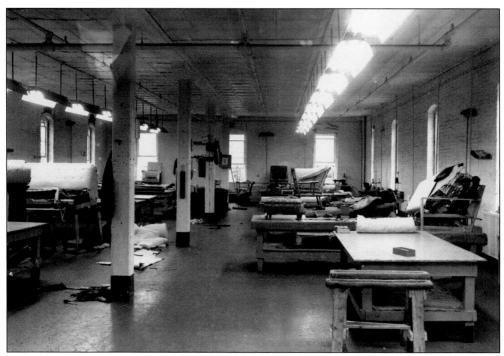

The USDB upholstery shop was located in building 467 and later moved to building 470. The shop repaired and renovated such items as couches, davenports, footstools, chairs, and the like. Mattresses, custom or standard sizes, were made or renovated, and custom seat covers were installed in automobiles. Antique furniture was a specialty of this shop. In the picture below, inmates repair uniforms to include shirts, pants, and coats.

The USDB photograph tag shop was located in the basement of building 472 and provided theoretical and practical training in developing, printing, enlarging, copy work, oiling, toning, cropping, and touching up of photographs and portraits. On June 4, 1957, equipment and supplies for license tags were received from Fort Gordon, Georgia.

The USDB shoe repair shop provided instruction and on the job training for the phases of shoe rebuilding and repair. Inmates could earn a vocational certificate of accomplishment. In 1996, a satellite shop was opened at the Fort Leavenworth Trolley Station called the "Cobbler's Corner." This shop provided repair services for all types of footwear and leather goods and "while you wait" repairs on some items. Customers still rave about the custom cowboy boots purchased from this shop.

The USDB sheet metal and welding shop was located in building 496 and provided training in all aspects of the sheet metal and welding trades. Inmates could earn a Kansas State Vocational Training Certificate and a certificate through the Department of Labor Apprenticeship Program. This shop fabricated items to support the entire USDB such as ductwork for various buildings and feeders for the farm colony. This shop specialized in customized projects to include large barbecue trailers and 30- and 50-gallon barbecue grills. In the picture at left, inmates are attending the 16-week long welding class.

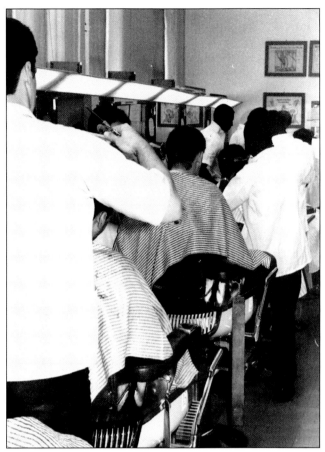

The USDB barbershop was located in building 467 and later moved to the basement of building 465. The barbershop taught inmates all phases of barbering to include cutting and shaping hair, shaving of necks and faces, application of tonics and oils, hair, scalp and skin ailments, electric and hand clippers, sanitary methods of operations, standard linen set ups, and shop management. Inmate barbers get plenty of practice since inmates are required to get a haircut every two weeks. In the picture below, staff and inmates are on a break at the back of building 467.

On October 31, 1963, building 470, a new vocational industries building, was dedicated at the USDB. James V. Bennett, director of the Federal Bureau of Prisons and commissioner of Federal Prison Industries (FPI) was the guest speaker along with Dr. Austin MacCormick, consultant to the secretary of the army on correctional matters. Approximately 200 inmates worked during various phases of the construction as plumbers, electricians, masons, and painters, as part of vocational training. The FPI furnished $350,000 of the $375,000 cost for the building. The building was later named after the third USDB commandant, Capt. James W. Pope (Pope Hall).

The USDB car wash and detailing shop were part of the Inmate Welfare Fund and were open to all personnel having a post decal on their vehicle. The shop was located across the street from the USDB and building 429, the barracks for the USDB soldiers. It was a popular location for customers to drop off their vehicles and shop at the USDB sales store. Because of force protection measures after the terrorist attacks on September 11, 2001, the shop was closed because of its close proximity to the soldiers barracks.

Six

FARM COLONY AND GREENHOUSE

The USDB farm colony or USDB farm was located approximately two miles northwest of the castle and consists of 470 acres of tillable soil. Vocational training was provided in the production of field crops, such as corn, milo, oats, and hay. A trusty inmate, under the hot Kansas sun, tills the land on Sherman Army Airfield with the USDB Castle in the background.

Pictured is an aerial view of the 2,400-acre USDB farm colony and its 12 major buildings. The land to the right side of the above picture is where the new USDB was built. In addition to vocational training in field crops, there was on-the-job-training and classroom vocational training in beef cattle, poultry, swine, horse stable management, heavy equipment operation, farm mechanics, and welding. There were an average of 30 trusty inmates employed at the USDB farm colony and they lived in building 424, the farmhouse. It closed in 1996 in preparation for construction of the new USDB.

Kansas is a rural state with farming as a mainstay. The USDB, like other older prisons in rural states, depended on farming to employ inmates and to offset the cost of feeding the inmates. Building 424 was the farmhouse also known as the Pony Express and is the only building that is still standing from this once busy colony. The land to the left of the USDB farm colony sign is under construction and is the future sites for the Joint Regional Correctional Facility, Fort Leavenworth, the 40th and 705th Military Police Battalion Headquarters (internment/resettlement), eight military police company headquarters, and two tactical equipment maintenance facilities.

The cattle enterprise was started in the spring of 1959 with these 33 open Hereford heifers received from the military prison at Lompoc, California. The plan was not to exceed more than a 100-cow herd by 1964. A year later, the Hereford herd consisted of 1 bull, 44 cows, and 16 calves. When the farm closed in 1996, 5 bulls, 144 cows, and 107 calves were sold.

The poultry enterprise consisted of laying hens, turkeys, pheasants, and quail. The turkeys, pheasants, and quail birds were raised and sold. In 1965, the laying stock of 3,500 hens produced an estimated 53,435 dozen eggs. Pictured below is a trusty inmate collecting eggs in the newly constructed 600 cage-nests egg processing building.

Building 358 was a wooden construction with a cement floor for swine operations. It was an 18-pen furrowing barn equipped with individual sow pens, automatic feeders and waterers, electric pig brooders, and inside and outside individual cement runs. In 1995, swine operations reported $48,205 in revenue.

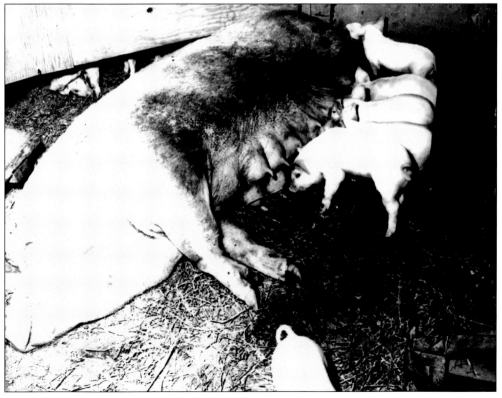

When the USDB farm colony first opened, it did most of its farming by hand or with livestock. New equipment was added to the inventory to keep pace with modern farm machines. A trusty inmate is making one more maintenance check before he operates a new Massey-Harris two-row corn picker. Pictured below is a John Deere, model 45, self-propelled combine.

The USDB farm metal sign mounted on wagon wheels supported by stone columns greets one as they enter the USDB farm colony on Kickapoo Road. Even though the farm no longer exists the sign was left intact as a historical marker of the past. The USDB farm colony operated a horse stable where military members could board their horses.

The USDB greenhouse was located midway between the USDB Castle and the farm colony and just north of the TU, formerly the LPU. The greenhouse was reported to have been the largest in the state of Kansas. The USDB greenhouse sales store was a three-story brick building built by inmates with inmate-made bricks. There were apartments located on the middle floor where some of the USDB staff resided.

The USDB greenhouse was the community's most popular USDB sales outlet. Inmates assigned to this detail received training in horticulture. It sold poultry, eggs, truck crops, and fruit produced by the farm colony. It also supported the Fort Leavenworth Directorate of Public Works' Self-Help Program, with 1,500 flats of bedding plants, shrubbery, 1,000 plants, and 20,000 fall bulbs for post beautification. The greenhouse closed on September 1, 1999, and the main structure was torn down on July 16, 2001.

The job of a correctional specialist at the USDB is not always about supervising inmates. This soldier is home on the range, moving cattle across the pastures of the USDB Farm.

Seven

KEEPERS

Military police who apprehend criminals are known as "Catchers" and the correctional specialists who confine them are known as "Keepers." Working behind the USDB walls was not for everyone. The stress associated with the unique environment of confining human beings against their will was tremendous. The most vivid memories were hot summers or cold winters walking through the courtyard with the thousand or more inmates during mass inmate movement.

The Directorate of Classification, later renamed the Directorate of Inmate Administration, was responsible for the inmate administration functions such as classification and clemency. Custody classification boards were held at least annually, and an inmate's rehabilitation progress, institutional behavior, and employment history was reviewed. Those inmates released from the USDB under the conditions of parole were managed by this directorate. Parole violators from all U.S. Army correctional facilities would return to the USDB.

As with any military organization, there is plenty of paperwork. The Directorate of Administration was divided into four divisions: administrative, management and budget, non-appropriated funds, and military personnel. The military personnel division was responsible for the maintenance and disposition of all military records for the soldiers of the First Guard Company.

A correctional treatment file, commonly referred to as a CTF, was established for each inmate assigned to the USDB. The CTF was the central depository for all paperwork associated with the inmate during his time of confinement. Some long-term inmates have volumes of CTFs, and on a daily basis, each file had to be inventoried and accounted for.

The most common way for inmates to communicate with the outside world was through the mail. It is also the most common means of contraband introduction into the USDB. Pictured here is an unidentified specialist fourth class inspecting incoming inmate mail with different mailbags for the delivery to the inmate housing areas. Phones were installed in the general population housing units for inmates to make "collect" calls only.

The USDB sales store was located to the left of the south gate entrance. It was the sales outlet for the products made by the inmates in the graphic arts, wood and sheet metal vocational shops as well as the inmate craft shop. Shoe repair and furniture upholstery were very popular but had been discontinued. In the above picture, a barbershop was located in the section of the building with the stairs.

The U.S. Army mandate was to provide education and rehabilitation opportunities to inmates. Those inmates at the USDB that did not have a high school diploma or a general equivalency diploma (GED) were enrolled in day school. A master sergeant is teaching a class to a group of inmates using the Finch Series World Products maps.

On July 8, 1955, Capt. James F. Neal, veterinary staff officer, points out a method of shaping a horseshoe to M.Sgt. Max McKinney, chief administrator and field NCO who doubles in the horseshoeing trade when needed at the USDB farm colony. Inmates were not the only ones who had an opportunity to learn new skills.

The main entrance into the USDB was commonly known as South Gate. Visitors for either staff or inmates were processed in at this location. To control the access inside the wall, a sally port with two sliding doors in the front and two sliding doors in the back were used. Except for special situations, a door from the front of the sally port was not to be opened at the same time as a door from the back of the sally port. Additionally the key and radio issue rooms were located here.

Pictured are soldiers on the third tier of a general population housing unit in one of the wings of the castle. This area was restricted access, and soldiers were required to check this area every 30 minutes and initial a form. A ladder connecting all of the tiers was located within this restricted area and was used during emergency evacuations.

There were 12 towers strategically located on the wall surrounding the USDB. A sergeant of the guard supervised the issuing of weapons and ammunition from the arms room and marched the service members to each tower and posted them. The towers were renovated with improved windows to increase the range of visibility and the ability to shoot from within the tower. An unidentified U.S. Marine is in three tower in 1989.

While married soldiers lived in family quarters like Bluntville, single soldiers lived in building 429, home of the First Guard Company, USDB Battalion, and later the 705th Military Police Battalion. Life in the barracks was similar to squad bay living in the rest of the U.S. Army. The picture below is of the dayroom where soldiers could go to relax and shoot some pool while enjoying a cold Coke.

On the first floor of building 429, the soldiers had their own mess hall. This provided them an opportunity to enjoy a meal without having to look over their shoulder to keep an eye on the inmates. Over the years, the mess hall was not cost efficient and was closed. Soldiers either consumed their meals at other mess halls on Fort Leavenworth or were authorized basic allowance for subsistence, commonly known as "separate rats."

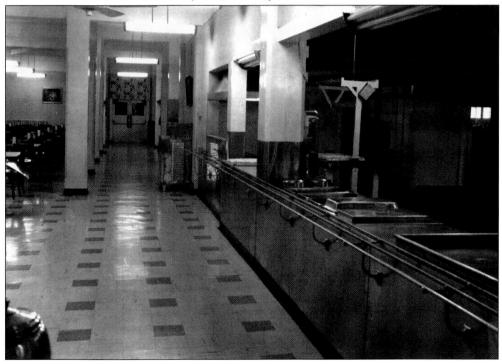

Between September 30 and October 5, 2002, using a prison bus from the United States Penitentiary Leavenworth, all the inmates were transferred from the old USDB to the new USDB. On Saturday, October 5, 2002, at 1322 hours, the USDB Emergency Operation Center sent the following e-mail message, "Mission complete, all inmates are secure and all routes are open. CMC Per Order CPT Washington." At 1700 hours, the same day, a flag detail led by S.Sgt. Barbara Fletcher retired the national colors from the old USDB for the last time. The colors are displayed in the showcase at the new USDB.

Eight

DESTRUCTION OF THE CASTLE

On April 5, 1994, the secretary of the army approved the building of a new USDB instead of repairing the USDB Castle after several structural studies were conducted on wind and seismic loads. This marked the beginning of the end for the castle.

Safety is one of the top priorities during a demolition. Asbestos had to be removed and encased prior to being shipped to a disposal facility. Several federal and state law enforcement and correctional agencies were allowed to salvage detention doors, sinks, and toilets unique to a prison.

The one-wing stairwell was the main staircase used to access the chapel and other administrative areas on the second and third tiers. The concrete stairs were noticeably worn from the number of inmates and staff over the past 70 years.

Both a 3,000-pound and a 6,000-pound wrecking ball were used to destroy the brick walls of the castle. The wrecking balls were used instead of implosion to reduce the risk of damage to the other historical buildings within the USDB walls. The public thought they were going to see an implosion similar to casinos in Las Vegas.

Despite attempts to retain the USDB Castle, demolition started on August 17, 2004. A USDB Adaptive Reuse Study was conducted with several options, including an urban training center, a records storage facility, or a convention center. Some thought it would have been an excellent lodging source for military students attending the Combined Arms and Services Staff School. Others thought it a great idea for a morale, welfare, and recreation bed and breakfast, with all-inclusive ghost stories.

Five wing was the first to be destroyed. On the top floor was the gymnasium with basketball, volleyball, and boxing equipment. In the middle was the dining facility with kitchen, food storage, and dining areas. On the second tier were the weight room, recreation and law libraries, and the music room. On the first tier were the supply and mailroom operations.

The castle foundation was reinforced concrete and the first two tiers consisted of white reinforced stone while the remaining six tiers were constructed with bricks made by the inmates. Since five wing was the dining facility area, some say to maintain the food service standard of "first in-first out," it was the first wing to be destroyed because it was the first wing built.

Special heavy demolition equipment was used to destroy the castle such as this mobile crane with a 220-foot boom and wrecking ball. As the wrecking ball smashed into the castle, water was sprayed onto the area to reduce dust exposure to the surrounding community. The below view is from the foundation of building 496 where the sheet metal and welding vocational shop was located.

This view is from the rooftop of the four wing, the medium-custody, general inmate population housing unit during the demolition of six wing. Four tower and five tower can be seen on the wall. Five tower was used to monitor inmate movement from the castle to the recreation field outside the north wall. Each tower was equipped with a powerful spotlight on the roof to illuminate the many shadowed areas inside the walls.

This is a view of six wing of the castle with exposed six tiers of cells separated with a utility corridor (pipe chase) between them. Six wing was the minimum custody housing unit with over 200 single and multiple occupancy cells.

Among all the rubble and debris is a pile of hardened china toilets from the inmate's cells. Most of the sinks and toilets that were salvageable were extracted so they could be used in local, state, or federal jails or prisons. Most of the older maximum custody prisons used separate harden china sinks and toilets, but most new prisons use a standard stainless steel sink/toilet combination for security and safety.

The third housing unit to feel the weight of the wrecking ball smashing into its wall was four wing. Four wing was a medium-custody, general inmate population housing unit and confined approximately 240 inmates in single cells.

This view portrays the center of the castle exposed, showing the interior of the rotunda's dome. The top of the dome had about 100 light bulb sockets and when illuminated could be seen for miles across the river in Missouri.

As each wing was destroyed, the castle's rotunda fought to stay intact. The castle was a hub-and-spoke design with the rotunda as the central hub with eight radiating wings. There were approximately 300 prisons worldwide that used this design.

Among all the destruction to the different wings of the castle, one of the wing's exterior fire escapes remained intact. Safety was important at the old USDB; monthly fire drills were conducted with the inmates and staff using either primary or secondary fire evacuation routes, including the one shown here.

The "USMP"-stamped bricks were made by prisoners at the brick plant on Fort Leavenworth. Sheets of clay were cut into brick size, and every 12th brick was stamped. These bricks were used to build the castle and other buildings in the prison and on Fort Leavenworth. Before renamed in 1915, the USDB was called the United Stated Military Prison. It has been estimated over 6.5 million bricks were used to build the castle. The bricks along with other debris were taken to a landfill. Some bricks were salvaged and distributed as souvenirs for USDB and Fort Leavenworth staff.

Pictured are two different aerial views of where the most dominant building on Fort Leavenworth once stood. The above view is from the west and the below view is from the north. For those who worked inside the walls of the old USDB, many are still perplexed on the idea the castle was able to fit into such a small space.

Pictured is an aerial view from the north of the old USDB with the Missouri River on the east and the bell tower of the headquarters, combined arms center, and Fort Leavenworth in the background. In the 1980s, as a young correctional specialist, the author escorted prisoners from the Fort Knox Installation Detention Facility to the USDB. While driving from the airport, the prisoners would joke about when they get inside the USDB, they were going to run the joint. After getting closer to the Missouri River where they could see the castle inside the USDB perched high on the ridge, the chatter in the vehicle went silent. The prisoners knew they were going to the "big house." Today a parking lot is located on the castle's historical ground.

Nine

A NEW
STATE-OF-THE-ART
FACILITY

The groundbreaking ceremony for the new USDB was held on June 12, 1998, with the keys handed over to Fort Leavenworth on August 1, 2002. After training and certifying the staff, the process to transfer the staff and inmates to the new facility began. At 1322 hours on October 5, 2002, the last inmates were secured inside the new USDB, thus ending the occupation of the old USDB. It took approximately eight years and six months to complete the mission after the secretary of the army directed a new USDB be built.

The USDB is located on the northern part of Fort Leavenworth on the site of the former USDB Farm Colony. The USDB consists of approximately 37 acres and 11 buildings, including 4 buildings inside double 12-foot perimeter fences. The perimeter has no security towers but is monitored by armed security patrols.

Seen here is the entrance to the main multipurpose building which contains food service, education, chapel, medical and dental clinics, central control center, visitation, vocational training shops, laundry, gymnasium/recreation areas, laundry, administrative offices, and the special housing unit.

The USDB encourages visits by family and friends to maintain the morale of the inmate and to develop closer relationships between the inmate and family members. The general population contact visitation room is open daily for visitation. The non-contact visitation booths are used for inmates in maximum custody, under a sentence to death, and those inmates who have lost the privilege of contact visitation. A wall and glass window separate the visitor from the inmate and a telephone is provided for verbal communication.

There are three general inmate population housing units designed as a bow tie with 140 single cells arranged linearly on the outer walls. The bow tie is divided into two housing pods separated by an enclosed control center. Each housing unit has an open center area containing pay phones, televisions, tables, and chairs. Large floor fans were replaced with a central climate control HVAC system.

Individual showers are a quality of life improvement from the group showers in the old USDB. The correctional staff can still observe the inmates showering, while the half door provides the inmate with privacy.

For safety and security, all general population cells were designed to be single occupancy with natural light from an exterior window, hot and cold running water, writing surface with stool, and a bed. Each cell has an intercom for communication to the correctional staff in the housing unit control booth.

The Directorate of Pastoral Care is responsible for the supervision of the religious programs consisting of over 35 identified inmate faith groups with 43 weekly services. The chapel shown can be neutralized to accommodate the different faith groups.

The USDB sports program has both indoor and outdoor sports for the inmates to participate in as an individual or as a team. The gymnasium consists of a weight room, basketball, volleyball, and handball courts. On July 17, 2003, the gymnasium was dedicated in honor of Sgt.Maj. Henry Lee Cook, a former USDB operations sergeant. He was the first corrections noncommissioned officer inducted into the prestigious Sergeant Morales Club. Sergeant Major Cook was an avid basketball player and died of complications while playing basketball during a Tuesday lunchtime game with other USDB staff.

Outdoor sports recreation consists of softball, basketball, soccer, running track, and free weights. Competition through intramural programs and tournaments are conducted in all major sports such as volleyball, basketball, and softball. The outdoor recreation area is open daily for inmate use dependent on the weather.

The old USDB had 12 permanent security towers perched on the stone walls, but the new USDB has none. A mobile security tower is used as an observation platform during recreation times and can be placed at tactical locations during emergency operations.

This view is from inside the USDB secure perimeter from the main central control room, down the main hallway of the multipurpose building. The hallway is under constant supervision by a close circuit television system and depending on the inmate's custody level, he is either escorted or unescorted in this hallway.

The Directorate of Inmate Administration (formerly the Directorate of Classification) maintains a correctional treatment file on every inmate assigned to the USDB. Over the years, these records can become very large. Correctional treatment files of former inmate files are transferred to the record holding facility in St. Louis, Missouri.

The U.S. Army's mess hall era ended and was replaced with modern dining facilities. Quartermaster soldiers still prepare three hot meals daily for the inmates and staff following the U.S. Army Master Menu guidelines. The dining facility was designed with two serving lines with the tables in the dining area secured to the floor to prevent their use during a disturbance. Inmates are assigned to detail 44 as kitchen police (KP). The cooks provide an extra touch during the Thanksgiving and holiday seasons using their culinary arts skills.

This is the USDB laundry. Detail 27 serves both the USDB inmates and the Fort Leavenworth community with basic laundry and dry cleaning services. The inmates assigned to this detail learn a useful skill using these industrial-size washing machines, steam presses, and dry cleaning machines. Inmates have their clothing and bed linen washed weekly.

The USDB operates a vocational barber college, detail 10, and a customer service barbershop outside the USDB in Truesdell Hall. Inmates are required to maintain grooming standards per U.S. Army regulation. Inmates assigned to this detail can earn a vocational certificate in barbering and test for a Kansas barbers license. The USDB vocational barber college consistently maintains the highest scores in the state of Kansas during the licensure examinations.

The USDB textile repair, detail 28, is divided into a light textile section and a heavy textile section. Items identified as salvageable by the U.S. Army are sent to this shop for repairs, such as sleeping bags, rucksacks, combat vehicle crewman (CVC) helmets, GORE-TEX gear, coveralls, ponchos, wet weather gear, and interceptor body armor. All items repaired are laundered, inspected for quality workmanship, and packaged individually prior to shipment. The items are then returned to the U.S. Army inventory for reissue. Inmates assigned to this detail can earn a vocational certificate.

The USDB wood shop, detail 21, offers vocational training in woodworking and specialized training in computer assisted drafting, computer numerical control programming operations, furniture manufacturing, and finishing applications. Inmates assigned to this detail can earn a vocational certificate through the Bureau of Apprenticeship and Training, Department of Labor, for completing the cabinetmaking and millwork course.

The USDB sheet metal/welding shop, detail 9, offers an apprenticeship certificate through the Bureau of Apprenticeship and Training, Department of Labor. Inmates assigned to this detail are provided 10-week-long welding classes followed by 6,000 hours of on-the-job welding experience. The baker's racks and barbecue grills made in this shop are popular among soldiers and family members worldwide.

The USDB graphic arts shop, detail 12, is comprised of three departments: art preparation, screen printing (textiles and decals), and printing and engraving. Inmates assigned to this detail can earn an apprenticeship certificate through the Bureau of Apprenticeship and Training, Department of Labor. The graphic arts shop produces items such as vehicle registration decals, business cards, shirts, decals, engraved glasses, boxes, awards, banners, and memo pads.

The USDB embroidery shop, detail 22, makes nametapes for U.S. Army Reception Stations and for university and high school Reserve Officer Training Corps (ROTC) units. Its largest customer is the retention and recruiting organizations and provides many different styles of embroidered incentives, shipping all over the world. Inmates assigned to this detail can earn a vocational certificate.

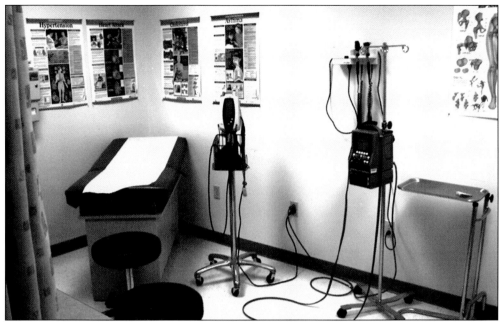

The USDB health clinic provides primary care, consulted specialty care, and on-call emergency services to the inmate population. The Fort Leavenworth Munson Army Health Center provides the military and civilian staff. The clinic capabilities include labs drawn, X-rays, eye exams, hearing tests, physical examinations, physical therapy, dietician, and orthopedic consults.

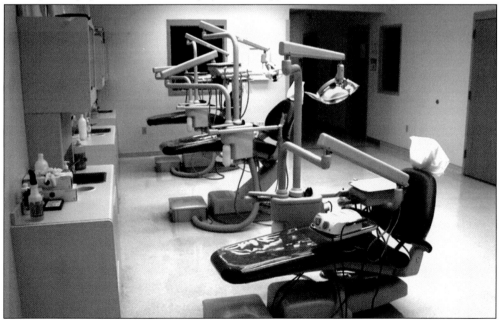

The USDB dental clinic provides dental sick call, routine procedures, annual exams, annual cleanings, and after hours on-call services for dental emergencies. The Fort Leavenworth Smith Dental Clinic provides the military and civilian staff. Inmates assigned to detail three can earn a dental assistant apprenticeship certificate through the Bureau of Apprenticeship and Training, Department of Labor.

The USDB West Gate is the portal for vehicle access into the facility and for in processing of new inmates sentenced to confinement at the USDB. The soldiers working here are the first line of defense in detecting contraband attempting to be introduced into the USDB. Inspections and searches of every vehicle are an inconvenience for the vehicle drivers but a requirement to ensure safety and security.

In less than one year of transition to the new USDB and through the efforts of the professional and dedicated civilian and military USDB staff, the Commission on Accreditation for Corrections and the American Correctional Association awarded accreditation to the USDB on August 11, 2003.

On September 30, 2003, Charles Kehoe, president of the American Correctional Association (ACA), presented the reaccreditation certificate to Col. Colleen McGuire, USDB commandant, and Lt.Col. Peter Grande, USDB chief of staff. The USDB's first ACA accreditation audit was in the fall of 1981 with the presentation of the certificate on January 22, 1982. The ACA is a professional membership association dedicated to the improvement of corrections and the training and development of correctional professionals. ACA accreditation provides the commandant with a tool for maintaining the USDB in accordance with nationally recognized standards for sound correctional practice and a mechanism for evaluating compliance with those standards. Accreditation ensures the USDB remains within the band of excellence while instilling pride and professionalism in all aspects of the corrections operation. This was not the first time the USDB or the U.S. Army had interacted with the ACA. In 1870, Maj. Thomas F. Barr attended the first meeting of the National Prison Association, later renamed the ACA, and the professional exchange of penal reform and correctional training has grown over the past 139 years. The active participation of the USDB commandants and staff is widely documented in the annual reports of the National Prison Association and the proceedings of the ACA's Congresses of Correction. Currently 15 USDB staff members are certified as correctional professionals from the Commission on Correctional Certification and the ACA.

Col. James W. Harrison Jr., a graduate of the United States Military Academy at West Point, New York, and a military police commissioned officer was the 47th USDB commandant from June 15, 2004, to June 21, 2006. On May 6, 2007, while serving as the director of Detainee Capabilities Directorate, Combined Security Transition Command in Afghanistan, he was killed in action along with M.Sgt. Wilberto Sabalu Jr., outside the Afghani National Detention Facility in Pul-i-Charkhi, Afghanistan. He is interred at the Fort Leavenworth National Cemetery, with grave marker K-152. On November 1, 2007, the road leading into the old USDB was dedicated in his honor.

Located at Fort Leonard Wood, Missouri, is the United States Army Military Police School and home to the Military Police Corps Regiment. The Military Police Memorial Grove offers a place for reflection, remembrance, and ceremony. The Military Police Regimental Walkway is made of bricks donated by organizations and individuals as a lasting tribute to the men and women of the Military Police Corps Regiment past, present, and future. The Military Police Regimental Association's Legacy Programs consists of the benevolent fund, scholarships and outreach, and the Military Police Regimental Walkway. The Military Police Regimental Association will receive the author's royalties from this book. Visit the Military Police Regimental Association online at www.mpraonline.org. (Courtesy Military Police Regimental Association.)

Discover Thousands of Local History Books
Featuring Millions of Vintage Images

Arcadia Publishing, the leading local history publisher in the United States, is committed to making history accessible and meaningful through publishing books that celebrate and preserve the heritage of America's people and places.

Find more books like this at
www.arcadiapublishing.com

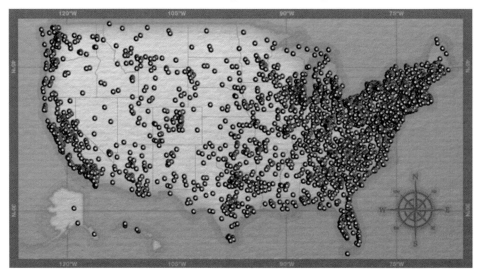

Search for your hometown history, your old stomping grounds, and even your favorite sports team.